"Tom Goodlet has laid out a very simple, yet powerful path for people to become more aware of who they really are, what they really want and how to begin making their hopes and dreams a reality. His personal anecdotes throughout are entertaining and make this book a pleasure to read. It's opened my eyes for sure."

Michelle Adams

Vice President, Gordon Training International

"Let's be honest... we've all heard that small voice inside us saying, "There must be more for me." Unfortunately, most of us don't know how to start uncovering our potential, or what the first step should look like. This book is that first step. *Blind Potential* is an enjoyable read, full of stories that will make you laugh and cry. Tom will also help you discover the best things hidden within yourself. Read this book and discover what more you have within."

Dr. Raul Serrano

Best-Selling Author of *The 14-Day Reboot*

Co-Host of the *Potentialist Podcast*

"Tom Goodlet's *Blind Potential* opened my eyes. I already knew he was an unrivaled communicator – as a speaker, motivator, and writer. By reading through his latest work I learned that the depth of his knowledge on our hidden potential can change our lives for the better if we take the time to soak it in. He's uncovered something powerful with this book."

Bobby Lewis

Five Time Emmy Award-Winning CBS Reporter

Author of *Finding Joy Beyond The Headlines*

BLIND

POTENTIAL

How to Clearly See Your Best Possible Self

Using Simple Steps to Guide You to a Purpose-Filled Life

TWO PENNY
PUBLISHING

DEDICATIONS

This book is dedicated to my beautiful wife Erica, who supports my dreams and calms my worries.

To my three kids Parker, Mason and Avri who keep me laughing, learning and make life a wonderful adventure.

And to my great circle of friends, especially Jodi, Raul, Adrian, Christian and a whole bunch of you listed in the Acknowledgments. Without you there would be no book. Thank you for blessing me. Now let this book be a tool to bless others.

TABLE OF CONTENTS

ACKNOWLEDGMENTS

Thank you:

... Jodi Costa for making this a book. As always, you do the most work and take the least amount of credit. The world has yet to fully realize your immense talent. Watch out world! Here is another major accomplishment by Jodi.

... Sarah Williams, Karen Hoke, Kim Roper, Wesley Dennard, Nancy Wyse, Erica Goodlet and Carol Goodlet for keeping my grammar in order, my words spelled correctly and my content understandable.

... Michelle Alexandre, Kurt Parker and the rest of the staff at Harborside Christian Church for cheering me on in these endeavors and encouraging me when I doubted my own potential.

... Adrian Traurig for your tremendous ability to take a crazy concept from my brain and turn it into a work of art.

... Dr. Raul Serrano for helping me shape this vision, prodding me on with excitement and paving some of the path for this book.

... Bryan Quimby for assisting me with the technical aspects for product sales and being an honest sounding board for idea refinement.

... Christian Hays for being a fan, a friend and always a positive promoter.

... Jeanmarc Alexandre for helping me with the website, the podcast and perfection.

... Bobby Lewis for swapping ideas and encouragement.

... Dr. Ben Spears for help with promotion and great marketing ideas.

...Valencia Rayner and Tom Goodlet Sr. for giving great first-reader's feedback.

... Dee Wilson for all the promotion, likes, shares, and encouragement on social media and in person.

... Harborside Christian Church for letting me pursue my dreams.

... Amy Traurig and everyone on the Facebook Book Launch Team for pushing to make this a better book. The Facebook Book Team includes Diana Journy, April Guardabascio, Melissa Planzo, Carol Burmood, Matt Gardner, Kandis Pinkstaff, Darren Scheaffer, Sarah Wybo, Joanna Frankenberry and Thomas Harmon.

1 HOW TO SEE WHAT YOU CANNOT YET SEE

Have you ever felt like there was more
to you than you could see or explain?

We all are loaded with potential whether we realize it or not. Most often, the problem is we do not realize how much potential is there, let alone accept the possibility of its existence. What if I could prove to you there is more potential within you than you can currently comprehend? It does not matter if you lean more towards confidence or insecurity, pride or humility, ambition or complacency. There is more in you than you know and more available to you than you can see. You will have to let go of any excuse popping into your head right now. You know, the type of excuse that tells you this book is not going to help you, this guy does not really know you, there is nothing more for you, you are too late or too early to start looking at more potential inside you, and so on. If you are willing to let these excuses go, if you are willing to read on, if you are willing to give this a try, then I will help you see what you cannot yet see. I want to guide you beyond your own blindness to your

Potential... once you
are able to see it,
you are
well on your way
to achieving it.

undiscovered potential. Because once you are able to see it, you are well on your way to achieving it.

Potential comes pre-packaged with passion. It is something undeveloped but still quite powerful. It is a possibility bringing with it an energy affecting anything and everything in its path. Your undiscovered potential is like a dragon sleeping in a cave guarding a treasure. Search the cave, awaken the dragon, find the treasure; and life will never be the same. For you it may be a skill, a goal, a deep passion or a dream lying dormant. It may be a possibility perfect for you, an opportunity waiting for you to claim, an inspiring venture with the power to change this world for the better. As scary as it sounds, it is time to find and wake the sleeping dragon, bend it to your will, ride it into victory, all the while releasing its power and claiming its treasure as your own. Don't know how to find these hidden dragons, your undiscovered potential? That is why I am providing the map. I will show you where and how to search. I will supply the right questions to ask and the simple steps to take. You will see what was hidden from you for too long. You will see what you cannot yet see. You will see new and great potential.

However, before we start focusing on you and your fantastic potential, you need to understand a little bit about me. Something happened to me in my early twenties that changed the trajectory of my life and taught me the principles and ideas I am about to share with you.

Potential comes
pre-packaged
with passion.
It is something
undeveloped but still
quite powerful.

SHARING A STORY

I had just graduated college. I started a new job and was renting my own apartment. I owned my own car. My parents and siblings lived in Virginia, but I was now living on my own in Tennessee. Life was exciting, life was hopeful, life was good. As I moved through this new stage of life and this new stage of independence, I noticed my prescription glasses were not quite cutting it for me. For most of my life up until this point, I had 20/20 vision. Recently, I started wearing prescription glasses for distance, but only in classroom settings to better see the chalkboard or whiteboard, or to wear on occasion when driving. I knew it had been a while since I visited the eye doctor. I assumed it was time to upgrade my prescription. So, while visiting my family in Virginia, I scheduled an eye appointment with a local optometrist. The eye exam commenced. Halfway through, the optometrist became visibly concerned. He could correct my vision back to about 20/40 with lenses; but for some unknown reason, that was the best he could do. The optometrist recommended I get a second opinion, so, I did. The second optometrist referred me to an ophthalmologist, who sent me for tests to rule out a brain tumor. What was once an exciting time in my life quickly became one of the scariest. Right away, several tests were done at hospitals to rule out cancer. While the cancer-free results offered relief, there was still the unsolved problem of my decreased vision.

> Ironically, I found myself hoping for poison.

I underwent even more uncomfortable and awkward tests as doctors poked, prodded and scanned my eyeballs. Eventually, I went to Vanderbilt University where I was diagnosed with a macular dystrophy called Aconedystrophy. This diagnosis simply meant the center of my retina, my macula, in each eye was diseased or damaged. The doctors told me this disease would increasingly and permanently affect my reading and driving. In other words, I could squint all I wanted; but my vision was not going to get any clearer for me. The more I tried to focus my eyes, the blurrier images became. I would have to rely more on my peripheral vision in order to see clearly. If the diagnosis was correct and it was in fact a disease, then the cone cells in my macula would get progressively worse over the years. The doctors also offered up the idea the diagnosis may not be one hundred percent correct. There was a chance my maculas were damaged one time due to something unknown, something poisonous to my eyeballs. Perhaps this poisoning did permanent damage to my maculas, but the condition would not get any worse. Ironically, I found myself hoping for poison.

A couple decades later, I am still rooting for poison. So far, eye doctors have been able to prescribe glasses returning my vision to 20/40. While I am grateful my vision has not terribly worsened, it still requires major and minor life adjustments to overcome what I cannot see. I still struggle to read subtitles on movies or sports scores in the corner of the television screen. I cannot see fast food menus displayed up and across the counter. When driving, I cannot always read the details of the exit sign in time to clearly determine if it is the exit I am supposed to take.

This may also explain why some people who don't know me very well might be offended when they wave at me from across a lobby or large room, and I seemingly ignore them. Though I might see them waving, I cannot make out the details of their faces. So, I will fake it and say, "Hey Buddy," or "How ya doing, man? Oops, I mean ma'am." The reality is, I'm not purposely ignoring anyone or trying to be rude; I simply cannot clearly see people from that distance.

Now that you know the limitations of my direct vision, let me share with you three things I learned that enabled me to see better and clearer than ever before. A little known fact about problems is that they inherently release potential. Problems allow for possibilities which were not present or evident before. It is often times of desperation which cause innovation, which then leads to inspiration. It is getting around, over or under obstacles which creates a fantastic amount of understanding.

First, because I cannot see objects clearly by viewing them straight on, I have learned more and more to see life through my peripheral vision. I literally see life more clearly from different angles. This has given me a heightened awareness of both my surroundings and myself. I see life in ways most people never take time to see. My eye condition has taught me I am not the only person with a problem or disadvantage in this life.

Secondly, everybody has some sort of problem and disadvantage, something they were not expecting to deal with in this life. That is why we need each other to navigate this world and more clearly see ourselves and the potential within.

Thirdly, I learned no matter how well I can see myself and no matter how well others can see me and relay pertinent information, there are still times I must move forward in a step, shift or leap of faith. I must move forward regardless of what my eyes cannot see, trusting in what my head, heart and gut know to be true.

Within these three lessons, there are three key principles that, when put into practice, will allow you to see what was once unseen. What was once undiscovered will become your clear potential on its way to being achieved. In these next pages, I will unpack these concepts into more practical knowledge and personal steps for you to take. If you dare, prepare to step, shift or leap forward into the truth of who you are and who you are meant to be. Get ready to see through your own blindness. Get ready to see what is undiscovered and undeveloped yet ready to become unlocked and unstoppable. Get ready to unleash your potential.

CHAPTER 1 SIMPLE STEPS:

1. Write down your answers to the following questions:

Why did you pick up this book?

_____

_____

What excites you the most about moving forward?

_____

_____

_____

2. Think about events in your life that did not go as you planned and yet taught you tremendous lessons you will always remember.

Name the events and the lessons.

EVENT   LESSON LEARNED

_____ _____

_____ _____

3. When you hear the word "potential," what comes to mind?

_____

_____

_____

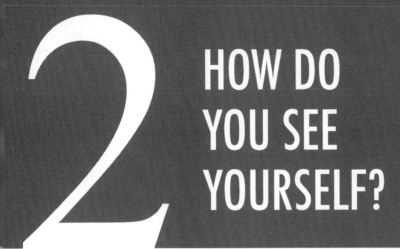

2 HOW DO YOU SEE YOURSELF?

Do not answer right away.
It is important to take some time to dig a little
deeper when answering this question.

The better and more accurately you can answer this question, the more hidden potential is revealed. In order to better answer this question, it helps to get outside of yourself, to try to see yourself from the perspective of an outsider looking in. Try to view yourself from different angles, like using a set of mirrors in a dressing room, viewing every side of yourself. Even the sides of yourself you do not normally see or in many cases care to see. Attempt to answer the question, "Who am I, really?"

THE VOICES IN MY HEAD

Before we answer the question, "Who am I, really?" it is important to acknowledge something. The first voices in your head are most likely incorrect or highly inaccurate, with the messages they try to convey to your conscience.

Why? Because the voices in your head are rarely your friend. Think about it. How often does the internal voice in your head build you up, encourage you and tell you there is nothing to get upset over or worry about? Most often, the voices in your head are keeping you down rather than

> **The voices in your head are rarely your friend.**

building you up. They are the voices who will spend their time answering the question "Who are you?" by telling you "Who you are not."

These internal voices place you at a disadvantage when trying to see your undiscovered potential. The voices in your head supply you with an abundance of fear, doubt, worry, and despair. They deliver lies into your head and tell you, "It's too late to try." "You should have started years ago." "You missed your chance." Your internal voices will even switch to lies telling you, "You are not ready, you need to wait." "You need more experience." "You are ill-qualified." Which is it? Is it too late or too soon? The truth is neither, because right now is your perfect opportunity. However, if you allow these voices to continue speaking loudly in your head, then you will soon feel frustrated, worrisome, stressed, depressed and hopeless.

In order for you to properly see who you really are, you must be careful with what you allow yourself to hear and what messages you allow into your heart. While the internal voices will continue to make their opinions known, you do not have to listen. The voices in your head have not earned the right to speak. They have not demonstrated a level of care for you, your well-being and your potential that deems them worthy of your attention. Your internal voices are not looking out for your best interests and are often filled with negativity. Negativity does not equal intelligence, as some foolishly assume. It takes little learning and brain power to point out what is wrong or what is difficult. The reverse is then true. It takes the better part of intelligence and more energy to spot the positive, to spot the potential. If you want to see potential in yourself that has previously gone unnoticed, then you will need as much optimism as you can acquire.

If the prominent voice in your head begins to sound like an excuse or assumption, you are listening to the wrong voice. The voices in your head will do everything in their power to promote fear and doubt. Here is the bad news. There is no way to get rid of the voices of fear and doubt. Here is the good news. There are ways to deal with them. In other words, fear and doubt are coming along for the ride. They will be in the vehicle as you travel towards the revealing of your potential. You have the choice. You can place them in the driver's seat of the vehicle, the passenger's seat, the backseat, or you can stuff them in the trunk where they belong.

I think you know what I know. It is time to silence, or at least drown out, the voices in your head so you can focus on the real you and your real potential. Maybe for you that requires listening to some positive music. Maybe it means going for a walk or run. Maybe it means getting outside into the noise of nature. One of my favorite ways to drown out the lies of the pessimistic voices is to fill my head with truth. I believe in the power of the Scriptures in the Bible. I find no better way to fill my head with truth and wisdom than to read or listen to the Proverbs of the prosperous King Solomon, or the prayers

If the prominent voice in your head begins to sound like an excuse or assumption, you are listening to the wrong voice.

and Psalms of the warrior King David, or the teachings and stories of Jesus of Nazareth whose life and ministry changed the trajectory of history. There is truth to be heard; so do whatever you need to do to hear it. Maybe for you, a good way to silence the unfriendly voices is to simply seek solitude and silence. I know the quiet often helps me sort my thoughts and metaphorically lock down the internal negative voices within my own head. It is worth researching and trying out any practices that might help you drown out the negative internal voices.

YOUR NAME

Once you take the time to devalue and silence the wrong influential voices, you can focus your sight through an honest and positive evaluation of who you really are. Who are you, really?

Start with your name. What is your name? Is there any significance behind your name? What does your name mean to you? What do you think of when you hear your name said aloud?

I remember the day I learned why my younger sister Christy received her name. We were kids when my mom rummaged through some old boxes in the attic. She brought down some books she found and placed them in a stack on the kitchen table. First, mom presented me with the book *Of Mice and Men* by John Steinbeck. She explained it was a book about two friends, George and Lennie. This book meant a lot to my mother. She had fond memories of reading it as a child. Mom thought I might appreciate knowing some of the story's plot line. She explained that the two friends in the story had a deep friendship and a complementary relationship. She shared how Lennie was big and strong but also a bit slow or intellectually disabled. George, in the story, was smart. He looked out for Lennie knowing Lennie's innocence and challenges. Mom explained that as the story progressed Lennie finds himself in more and more trouble. And then mom could not help herself. She revealed the all-time spoiler. Maybe she did not want me to be too devastated, or maybe she knew the ending would compel me to read the book out of curiosity of the gruesome details of the tragedy. Mom softly shared that Lennie dies. Moreover, George is the one who feels he has to kill him in order to spare him from a worse death awaiting him. She warned me about the sad ending but explained it was still a story worth reading.

Then mom presented a book to my younger sister Christy. The book was *Christie* by Catherine Marshall. Mom explained to my sister how this was a story about a beautiful girl who had a strong Christian faith. Her faith and devotion to God got her through some rough times. No matter the trials she faced, Christie shined as an example of someone blessed by God. My mom went on to explain how this book influenced her so much that she named my sister Christy.

That is about the time it hit me. When Mom thinks about my sister Christy, it reminds her of a story about a beautiful young lady who had a powerful faith in God that allowed her to overcome life's obstacles. And when Mom thinks about me, it reminds her of a story about a mentally challenged guy who keeps getting into trouble so much so they have to shoot him in the head. Hmmmmm.

I am not sure what my mother was trying to communicate in those moments, but needless to say there is power and thought that goes into a name. What are thoughts behind your name?

SHARING A STORY

I remember the day when my two boys figured out my true name. They were quite young when they came up to me with proud smiles on their faces, like they just solved one of the toughest mysteries of the universe. They said to me, "We know your real name. We know your real name is not Daddy." I answered, "Oh you do, do you?" They answered back, "Yeah. We know your real name is Uncle Tom." That is when I realized that the only time they heard me addressed not as Daddy was by their cousins. I humorously replied to my boys, "Congratulations! You figured it out, but now you have to keep it a secret."

What are some of your other names? Father? Mother? Husband? Wife? Uncle? Aunt? Cousin? Sibling? Co-worker? Friend? Neighbor? Boss?

Which parts of your name more strongly define who you are? I teach my kids to remember who they are as represented in their last name. I tell them, "We are Goodlets. This means we help people, we have fun and we honor God." At random times in their lives I quiz them and see if they remember the three things it means to be a Goodlet. By the way, we chose these three things as part of our family mission statement. This has been the explanation of why we go to church, why we sponsor a child in Africa, why we give away clothes and toys to the poor, why we make sure to have family time, why we play games together, and why we hug people who are crying.

A few years ago, our kids were out playing and riding bikes with one of the neighbor girls. The neighbor girl for some unforeseeable reason took a spill off her bike and bloodied her knee. As her parents ran towards her screams, my oldest son, Parker, ran into our house, grabbed a neon green bandage with antiseptic on it and ran it back out to the young girl. For the rest of the day they played together, and the little girl wore her bright neon green bandage over her wound. Later, I pulled Parker aside and told him how proud I was of him for helping out the neighbor girl. He simply replied back to me, "I'm a Goodlet and Goodlets help people."

What does your name say about you? Or better yet, what would you like your name to say about you?

YOUR DESIGN

Once you have wrestled with some of these questions, it is time to go beyond your name to something a little more detailed, your design. Who are you? What traits and aspects when properly put together make up you? What is your design? In our book MentorU, co-author Matt Gardner and I built a foundational framework of understanding between mentor and mentee by exploring each individual's DESIGN.

Understanding your DESIGN can assist you in exploring how you see yourself. The word DESIGN is an acrostic which stands for your Desires, Experiences, Skills, Ideals, Gifts and Nature. Take some time to walk through your DESIGN and answer the following questions. Stay positive. It is okay if some of your answers feel a bit out of reach:

DESIRES:

What are you passionate about? What would you love to do more often if you were able? What are your top three to five dreams for your future?

EXPERIENCE:

What are some past achievements that open up doors for your future? What are some past hurts, disappointments and lessons learned that could be used to open up avenues for potential future successes?

SKILLS:

What talents and abilities come naturally to you? What current strengths or skills would you love to develop to the next level?

IDEALS:

When you look at the world around you, what breaks your heart or makes you angry? What beliefs or values do you have that are unwavering?

GIFTS:

What abilities, resources or circumstances do you currently have that seem more like blessings than deserved rewards? If you could excitedly give something back to this world, what would it look like?

NATURE:

How would you describe your personality? This would be a fantastic opportunity to seek out and take a personality test. If you want to see potential within yourself then it will help to see some of the potential that is prewired within your own personality.

YOUR IDEAL YOU

Once you take a little time to see yourself from a different angle, you start scratching the surface of who you are. The next question to ask is "Who do you want to be?" To answer this question, you will need to look at yourself from another angle.

What does the ideal you look like? Picture the ideal version of you. Start by exploring how the ideal you is dressed and the type of body shape the ideal you has acquired. More importantly, dive into this line of questioning:

What is the ideal facial expression of the ideal you? Are you happy? Peaceful? Hopeful?

Is your facial expression the result of something you have accomplished, something you are regularly doing, or something which you have left behind?

What does the ideal you do with your time?

What kind of relationships does the ideal you have?

How does the ideal you contribute to the world?

What kind of legacy has the ideal you built?

Take some time to answer these questions and others. Remember, if you start doubting, making assumptions and excuses or thinking negatively, you are listening to the wrong voice. Stay positive. Your potential is waiting to be discovered.

How you see yourself is not just about seeing who you are; it is about seeing and acknowledging who you can be. Potential is often found in the tension between the two pictures. So, if you see something you did not see before, then write it down. It may become a future goal or pursuit. It may become your reality before you even know it. If you answered these questions and discovered nothing new about yourself and your potential then try going back and digging a little deeper. Skip the obvious and reach for the obscure. See what possibilities you can uncover. See what potential you can find. If you still struggle to see new potential by observing and acknowledging how you see yourself, then it is okay to move on to the next chapter and see what undiscovered potential awaits you there.

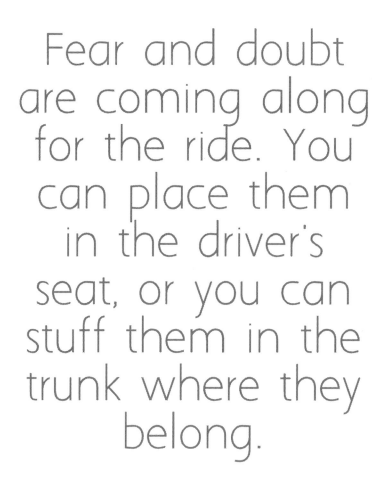

Fear and doubt are coming along for the ride. You can place them in the driver's seat, or you can stuff them in the trunk where they belong.

CHAPTER 2 SIMPLE STEPS:

1. List ways you will try to drown out any negative voices in your head.

_____

_____

2. While staying positive, ask yourself the question, "Who am I, really?" What positive thoughts come to mind?

_____

_____

3. Think about your name and what it may reveal about who you are.

What is your name? _____

Is there any significance behind your name? _____

What does your name mean to you? _____

_____

What do you think of when you hear your name said aloud? _____

_____

What are some of your other names (father, daughter, aunt, neighbor?)

_____

What does your name say about you? _____

_____

What would you like your name to say about you? _____

_____

4. Write down your answers to the questions below revealing your DESIGN.

DESIRES: What are you passionate about? What would you love to do more often if you were able? What are your top three to five dreams for your future?

_____

_____

EXPERIENCE: What are some past achievements that open up doors for your future? What are some past hurts, disappointments and lessons learned that could be used to open up avenues for future successes?

_____

_____

SKILLS: What talents and abilities come naturally to you? What current strengths or skills would you love to develop to the next level?

_____

_____

IDEALS: When you look at the world around you, what breaks your heart or makes you angry? What beliefs or values do you have that are unwavering?

_____

_____

GIFTS: What abilities, resources or circumstances do you currently have that seem more like blessings than deserved rewards? If you could excitedly give something back to this world, what would it look like?

_____

_____

NATURE: How would you describe your personality? This is your opportunity to seek out and take a personality test. To see potential within yourself, it is helpful to see the potential that is prewired within your own personality.

_____

_____

5. Write down your answers to these questions while picturing the ideal version of you. Use the space provided to write or draw your answer.

What is the ideal facial expression of the ideal you? Are you happy? Peaceful? Hopeful?

Is your facial expression the result of something you have accomplished, some thing you are regularly doing, or something which you have left behind?

What does the ideal you do with your time?

What kind of relationships does the ideal you have?

How does the ideal you contribute to the world?

What kind of legacy has the ideal you built?

_____

_____

_____

_____

_____

Draw the IDEAL YOU

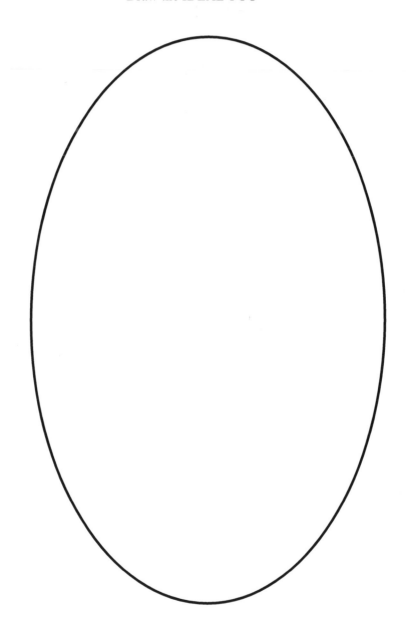

6. Note any possible goals revealed or potential steps you find within the tension of who you currently are and who you desire to be. Look for dragons worth riding. List your dragons.

_____

_____

_____

_____

_____

_____

_____

_____

3 HOW DO OTHERS SEE YOU?

Sometimes there is a knee jerk reaction to the question above: "It does not matter what anyone else sees or thinks about me."

This reaction stems from something experienced in life, where someone whose opinion you valued let you down. Everyone has been hurt from the wrong words delivered at the wrong time from the wrong person. It may even have been by a person who was trying to help you and instead made things worse. No one likes to be hurt. A common reaction is to avoid the possibility of hurt by not allowing anyone close enough to critique or disappoint you. Sometimes, it is easier to assume everyone around you is wrong, or foolish, or selfish, or just jerks waiting to hurt somebody.

SHARING A STORY

One day I was driving the whole family in our minivan—the "man van" is what I call it so I can feel better about driving it in public. Anyway, I was trying to get to the Home Depot about ten minutes from our home. I was on the main road in the middle lane of three heading in the direction of our destination. I put on my right blinker as I needed to turn soon. As I edged my way over into a gap between cars, the car in the right lane slightly behind me sped up so I could not merge. "What a jerk," I said in my head and probably out loud. He intentionally sped up when he knew I was trying to get over. I decided to show him I did not need his courtesies. I aggressively pressed down the accelerator and sped on ahead of him and several cars down when I spotted another gap in the right lane of traffic. As I began to merge into the right lane on my second attempt, the car in the right lane slightly behind me began to speed up like the driver before. But I would not be pushed out again, so I forced my way into the right lane and claimed my well-deserved position despite the opinion of surrounding drivers. As I showed off my *Fast and Furious* driving skills, the car behind me in the right lane laid on the horn. "What jerks," I said in my head and probably again out loud. Let's be honest for a moment, I might have said "jerk," but I probably had another word in my head as I wondered what was wrong with these people. That was about the time I noticed it. Because I was too busy proving a point, I did not take into view the flags on the cars that were now right in front of me, and the hearse a few cars ahead leading the trail of cars in the right lane. The realization of what I had just done hit me like a cold shower. I forcibly cut my way into a funeral procession. I looked for the first right hand turn I could make and got out of the procession as my kids wondered why those people in their cars looked so angrily at us. Sometimes when you think the world around you is full of jerks, you fail to realize you are the biggest jerk of all.

You and I need people to protect us from ourselves, people who will try to keep us from making major mistakes, or who will lay on the horn when we are not getting the message we desperately need to hear. You and I need people who can see what is going on around us when we cannot. We need people who want to help us discover and stay on the path that leads to our success. We need people who value us enough to help us see our potential and help us live it out.

AUTONOMY IS A LIE

Before dissecting how others see you as a method to uncover more potential within you, I want to address two obstacles that will withhold truth from you along your journey to discovering your potential. The first obstacle is the lie of autonomy. Autonomy is the idea that you do not need anyone else; you can fully stand on your own. It is easy and somewhat natural to pursue autonomy. People want to self-govern, individuals want independence, each person wants to be accountable to no one. While these ideas are not in themselves horrible, they are not completely attainable nor accurate in the happiness they advertise.

It is interesting to me that men, including myself, desperately chase autonomy. A man often wants to be his own boss, his own authority, his own independent man free from the support of others. The problem regarding autonomy is that it is a blatant lie. Even if you are the CEO, you are accountable to a board or shareholders. Even if you own your own business, you are accountable to your customers. Recently, a man who started his own business told me, "I decided to become my own boss, and instead I took on hundreds of bosses." He knew if he stopped pleasing his customers he would

Independence is
a myth.
Autonomy is
a lie.
Every someone
needs
someone else.

have no business left. Autonomy is a lie, because people will always need other people to succeed; and there is nothing wrong with this truth.

I find the timing of my eye condition no coincidence. The eye disease diagnosis all happened around a time in my life when I thought I would be fully independent. I had my own job, car, apartment and future plans. This was at a time in life when I was not supposed to need anybody anymore. My eye condition forced me to realize I would always need somebody to read me the subtitles or sports score when the tv was too far away. I would always need somebody to tell me what the fast food menu says across the counter. While driving, I would always need someone to let me know if my highway exit is coming up, because they would see it before I would. Just when I thought I was meant to be independent, I realized my future would always in some way depend on someone else.

The truth is, I am not alone in my condition and struggle because everyone on this planet has something—some condition or struggle—making people dependent on other people. Every someone needs to rely on someone else. You need people who will help you along the way and who will see in you what you cannot yet see.

THE LIE OF OBSERVATIONAL EQUALITY

The second obstacle to address when exploring the question "How do others see me?" is the lie that everyone's observation matters equally. Like the internal voices in your head, not every individual demonstrates a level of care for you that makes him or her worthy to be heard. If you have not grasped it by now, let me remind you potential requires positivity. Sure, you are going to need to listen when some people say what you would rather not hear, but the intentions and heart of those delivering the message must be measured before receiving the message into your own heart.

Think of it like sorting through junk mail or spam mail. Not every message deserves to be read. Look for optimism, for hope, and for wisdom from others to help you discover your undiscovered potential. Practice sorting through people's input so you will get better and better at knowing to whom you should give an ear and to whom you should ignore.

If you pursue your potential, you will attract critics. Reactions to your life pursuits usually start with people ignoring you as you chase after your dreams. Then those same people will laugh at you; and finally, they will fight you. If you remain strong against the scoffers and attackers, you will win. You will be too far ahead for your critics to land a fatal blow. You will shore up an inevitable victory.

I once heard that "Opinions are like armpits. Everyone has them and most of them stink." The farther you pursue your potential and the more potential you achieve, the more people feel the liberty to critique you and your efforts. You must be careful whose opinion you take to heart. It amazes me how the people who have never been in your role nor borne your responsibility often have the most to say. You want to learn from people with experience, people who have been there. If you won an NFL Super Bowl or an NBA Championship, there is a good chance you would be invited on national television to be a football or basketball commentator. Everyone wants to hear your evaluation and opinion of the game during halftime. You have

People will critique people who are doing something important rather than doing something important themselves.

then earned the right to be heard. What also amazes me is how little these experienced commentators tend to critique the players and coaches. Even they know it is not just what you say but how you say it, if it is worth being said in the first place. People who frequently critique others just have to get it off their chest so they feel better. People who critique because they care about the person to whom they are speaking restore and build people up more than they break them down.

It is amazing to me how many people will critique people who are doing something important rather than doing something important themselves. It is the critic who wants to be a part of something bigger than themselves. It is the critic who uses negative observation and speculation to try to achieve a false sense of personal accomplishment. One of my favorite illustrations of this type of behavior took place after the 2018 Super Bowl. Professional recording artist Pink sang the national anthem before the big game. It was communicated in earlier news reports that Pink had the flu and might not be able to perform. However, Pink pushed through her symptoms and misery to perform the national anthem. During some of the high notes of the song, it was apparent Pink was struggling to hit and hold the notes. Pink persisted and made it through the song with little damage, and the night went on. Later that night a random critic went to Twitter and tweeted, "If I've said it once, I've said it 1000 times. Pink sucks, and if you like her singing you're dumb." Pink decided to respond with a follow up tweet saying, "Yeah but at least I suck while singing our country's national anthem, and you just suck by yourself on a dirty couch." The observers in the stands do not earn the right to critique those on the field unless they themselves were once successful at the game. Be careful whose observation you accept.

THE WISE, THE FOOL AND THE EVIL

When figuring out whose opinion deserves a listen, it helps to understand there are two types of people in the world. There are those who generalize people into numbered categories and those who do not. I like that joke and I am about to be guilty of it.

A mentor once shared with me there are three types of people; the wise, the fool and the evil. A wise person values efficiency, creativity, the long term and you. My mentor explained that a wise person is capable of discussion even when the two of you disagree. In fact, the wise person is content to agree to disagree and feels better for having the discussion. The fool, on the other hand, will resent any lack of agreement between the two of you. The fool gets lost in the short term and tends to focus on his or her own insecurities and ego. The fool will be upset if you disagree and will not be able to get past it enough to learn from your perspective. Foolish people often try to engage the wise in annoying arguments. These are unwinnable arguments, because foolish people do not value reason or rationale. They simply are lost in their feelings at the time. You can lovingly rebuke fools in hopes they will become wise; however, most often fools will not understand nor see the benefit in the rebuke because they are fools. Fools will simply resent you.

Then, there are the evil. They just want to destroy you and the world around them. This reminds me of the movie *Batman the Dark Knight* and Heath Ledger's portrayal of the villain, the Joker. Throughout the movie, Batman tried to understand the Joker in order to defeat him. Eventually Alfred, Batman's butler, explained to Batman that some people are not meant to be understood. There is no reasoning with these men. They are pure evil. They just want to watch the world burn. My mentor's advice about the evil is to just avoid evil people at all cost because they only want to hurt you. The good news is lunatics never unite.

There is freedom in knowing you cannot have equal conversations with everyone. You have to identify which type of person to whom you are talking. If he is a fool, then it is easy to waste unnecessary time and energy trying to convince someone who will not be convinced nor willing to work it out with you. You can tell a fool that he is behaving like a fool, but he won't understand and often won't change because he is a fool. Be careful, because inside all of us, we all have some foolishness. It has been said that those who spend much of their time arguing with fools eventually become a fool themselves. The other two are easier, because it is never a good idea to associate with evil, and a conversation with the wise is never a waste.

> ... because inside of us, we all have some foolishness.

THE RIGHT PEOPLE

I learned I can love a fool and not expect him to be more than he is. It is disappointing because usually I care about the fool enough to want better for him or her. Most often it is the fool who did the most damage to me in my life. The only reason he could do so much damage is because I held him in higher regard and made myself more vulnerable to him or her than was needed. Don't trust a fool to be more than a fool. Don't lend an ear to a fool, accept his or her observations of you or put yourself in a position where the fool can continually abuse you. That would be foolish.

Now that you know to avoid the evil person and not to take the fool's views to heart, the next step is to know whose observations to take seriously. You need the viewpoint of wise people to help pinpoint your own potential. You will need someone wise ahead of you - who has gone before you, someone wise beside you and someone teachable behind you. You need the right people in place to make the right observations at the right, critical points of your life.

SHARING A STORY

Jay Jones saved me. It was about three years into my tenure overseeing a growing department within a stagnant organization. I was cynical, sarcastic and depressed. Most of this was due to poor leadership above me and, as I would soon learn, poor leading of myself. The organization had recently hired a new position which would oversee all the department heads, including myself. A new but experienced employee named Jay Jones accepted the position. For some reason, Jay took an interest in me and decided to invest himself in my future. Years later, when I asked him why he decided to invest so much in me, he shared he saw wasted potential and a young man with much talent lost in frustration. Jay was now my supervisor. He challenged me to read my first assigned book, *The 360 Degree Leader* by John Maxwell. This book changed my outlook and in turn, my life. Jay knew I was frustrated with the senior leader of the organization and had a hard time respecting and trusting him. Consequently, I felt demotivated. Jay knew what I needed to learn. The assigned book taught me that whether or not I would be a great leader was not contingent upon the guy above me or even at the top of the organization. It was my decision alone that mattered. While reading the book, I decided I would be a great leader no matter where my name appeared on the organizational chart. As the book taught, a great leader leads well to those below, under his or her supervision. A great leader also leads across to his or her colleagues no matter the colleagues' thoughts or behaviors. A great leader leads above him or her no matter the quality of the boss' oversight. This meant I could lead well no matter my circumstances. I could even help the senior leader by leading up to him. This meant that I could help the senior leader accomplish what the organization needed most by taking initiative, dealing with potential problems before they manifested into larger dilemmas and keeping the leader above me informed. No longer did the differences between the senior leader and myself depress me; but rather they provided opportunity to learn, be stretched and lead well. *The 360 Degree Leader* was just the first of many assigned readings and follow-up discussions as Jay Jones poured his life and experience into mine. I am forever grateful Jay empowered me. He was one of my unofficial and highly influential mentors. Jay and I are still friends and I still value his observations and input.

SOMEONE BEFORE YOU

You need a mentor. You need someone who has gone ahead of you or before you in life and who knows the obstacles coming your way. You need someone in front of you who can spot potential within you. This can be a difficult relationship to start and develop, which is why I co-wrote a book on how to begin a mentorship.

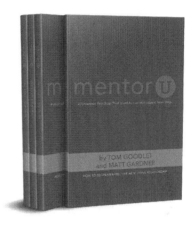

MentorU is available on Amazon. When you are in any form of leadership, having a mentor or two or three is key.

SHARING A STORY

A couple years ago my family got season passes to an amusement park and its adjoining waterpark. The waterpark made the Florida summer heat more bearable. There were several waterslides that all three of our kids could enjoy. And then there was that one slide that stood apart from the rest. It is the slide that most waterparks have. It is super-tall; and it drops straight down, thus creating a force of nature and science where one's bathing suit finds its way up and into one's lower intestines. I call it "The Wedginator." Because this slide is an extreme thrill ride, there are height requirements for its riders.

I have two sons with two vastly different personalities. Parker is the oldest and he tends to be more cautious when considering trying something new.

Mason is two years younger and he likes to find out how things work after he has jumped head first into them. As the summer progressed, Mason begged me to let him ride "The Wedginator." I explained that he did not yet meet the height requirements nor was he going to before the summer was over. Parker, on the other hand, grew enough to meet the height requirement in time for our last summer visit to this waterpark. On that visit, I revealed to Parker he was now tall enough to ride the slide if he so desired. To be clear, Parker never once asked all summer if he could ride that slide. I was just curious if he would consider it. Consider it he did. The rest of the day he wrestled with the idea of whether or not he wanted to try this extreme ride. It was the end of the day when he decided it was time for him to give "The Wedginator" a try. I explained to Parker that, while I could go up all the staircases to the top alongside him, he would have to go down the slide by himself. Parker and I climbed up and up and up until we reached the top platform where we could feel the wind swaying the metal tower-like structure back and forth. I excitedly went down the slide first, leaving Parker at the top looking down. The rest of the family waited at the bottom of the slide to see if Parker would go through with it. Sure enough, he came flying down the slide, ending in a big splash and the guaranteed wedgie. After snotting out all of the water he inhaled, he exclaimed, "I am doing that again!" Parker ran back up the stairs to slide again as Mason watched from below, longing for the day when he would be tall enough to ride.

While mentorship is beneficial for everyone, not everyone is ready for mentorship.

This dynamic reminds me of mentorship. While mentorship is beneficial for everyone, not everyone is ready for mentorship. Just because you want to do it does not mean that you meet the requirements of being ready. Just because you meet all the requirements does not mean you have the resolve to take the necessary steps with the courage to try the ride. Mentorship has both requirements to meet and resolve to implement. You know you are ready for mentorship when both mentor and mentee meet the requirements and you are willing and excited to give it a whirl. Then it becomes an extreme thrill ride worth doing again and again.

SOMEONE BEHIND YOU

I had thought about it for a while, months actually. I had thought about who I should mentor. Because I had a few mentors ahead of me in life, I knew it was my responsibility to find someone behind me, someone who I could mentor. It was not an obvious answer right away. The people who were consistently seeking my attention were not jumping onto my list in my mind as great candidates. I had to look around my life and soon it became clear and confirmed. Jared was the clear choice. CLEAR is an acrostic used in *MentorU* to help you know how to look around and select a good candidate for the mentor relationship.

C - connect
L - learn
E - excited
A - authentic
R - reliable

When broken down it's someone with whom you naturally Connect, someone who can Learn from you, someone who would be Excited to be in a mentor relationship with you, someone who is Authentic, and someone who is Reliable. Jared and I easily connected. He was easy to talk to and genuinely interested in his future as well as interested in my life. I knew Jared could learn some principles and skills from me. I knew I could help him in communication, teaching and leadership. These were all key components in my success. I was excited at the chance to pour into Jared, if he would let me, because I knew it would not go wasted. Jared had upcoming opportunities to practice what he would learn and expand his influence. I also observed him putting advice I previously gave him into practice. Jared was authentic. He was real with himself and honest about where he was in life. These were key components if he and I were going to dig deeper into his life, skills and challenges. If he was not real with himself, then he would have to peel those layers of the onion outside of mentorship and do some therapy or soul searching. He needed to be real with himself. Jared was also reliable. I could always count on him. So, if we were going to set up a time, I knew he would take it seriously.

Overall, I saw potential in Jared. It was the type of potential I knew Jared could not yet fully see within himself. I was slightly ahead of Jared in life. He would be the person behind me that I could pour into. I nervously asked Jared if he would be interested in a mentor relationship with me, fearing possible rejection. He excitedly exclaimed, "Yes!" And the mentorship journey began.

The benefit of having someone behind you in life is that you discover new potential in your own life while then being given the opportunity to test it

You are fed
more when you
are feeding.

out. As a mentor, you grow fast. You are fed more when you are feeding. As a mentor, you have access to direct feedback. You see how effective your skills and abilities are when helping another achieve their potential. As you look to spot undiscovered potential in the mentee, it reveals maps of hidden places of potential within yourself. By helping someone behind you, you multiply your life efforts and create potential colleagues who are in line with your vision. You expand your own cheering section as you pursue your dreams. Mentoring someone provides meaning, purpose and legacy for your life. Mentoring someone changes the world for the better.

SOMEONE BESIDE YOU

If you set up people in your life before you and behind you, you still need someone beside you. You need people next to you who see potential in real time as you see it. You need people beside you who have your back, people who see more than oncoming problems, people who see oncoming opportunities. Wise friends see and warn you about the potential dangers that threaten your most important opportunities, because they care about the quality and success of your life. You need someone beside you to encourage you and to help protect you. You need the honesty, the accountability and the wisdom of someone beside you.

Ryan Bailey has been my friend for years. He has been my partner in accountability for almost a decade. Ryan texts me on a weekly basis to see how I am doing, and he expects an honest

> You need the honesty, the accountability and the wisdom of someone beside you.

answer. He knows my strengths well. Ryan also knows my weaknesses. I also know his abilities and vulnerabilities. Ryan and I have breakfast together once a month. We chat face to face about our struggles, life trials, goals and celebrations. The irony of our accountability relationship is that the more open and vulnerable we are with each other, the stronger our respect for each other grows.

Ryan once shared with me what a "bailey" is. A bailey is the defensive wall surrounding an outer court of a castle or the courtyard itself. In other words, the bailey is the outer perimeter of defense or, at worst, the area between the two defensive walls. It is a strategic element to any castle harboring great treasure. The bailey's goal is to preserve and protect that which is most important held within the barriers of protection. That person beside you helps you stay on the path in pursuit of your potential. He speaks truth into your life as you both travel along the journey together. The wise person beside you helps you preserve your dreams and passions. He helps you identify and protect your potential. The wise person beside you is a perimeter defense the opposition has to find a way around in effort to destroy you. The people beside you are often your best friends. Ryan continues to be one of my best and most trusted friends. Ryan Bailey is literally my "bailey."

When you're ready to discover new potential within yourself, then you need to hear how others see you. Not just any "others." The right kind of "others." The kind of "others" who can see you and your life from different angles and call out the potential they spot. These are wise people who can provide insight from their unique perspectives of you. They are the people you have acknowledged or placed before you, behind you and beside you. They earned the right to share what they see. These wise and teachable, strategically-placed people in your life will ensure you will see what you cannot yet see.

These wise
and teachable,
strategically-placed
people in your life
will ensure you will
see what you
cannot yet see.

CHAPTER 3 SIMPLE STEPS:

1. What positive observations about you have others shared with you?

_____

_____

2. Think about the people who helped you get this far. What are their names? How have they benefited you?

NAMES   BENEFITS

_____   _____

_____   _____

Would it be beneficial to pursue a further relationship with any one of them at this stage of your life? Why?

_____

3. Think about your current relationships, friendships and acquaintances. Include those you would like to get to know better. Next to the list of names of wise people, identify who is (or could be) before you, beside you and behind you.

NAME

_____	Before	Beside	Behind	(circle one)
_____	Before	Beside	Behind	(circle one)
_____	Before	Beside	Behind	(circle one)

4. Fill in the grid with those currently behind, beside, and before you.

BEHIND	BESIDE	BEFORE
_____	_____	_____
_____	_____	_____

Observe any gaps in your grid. Who can you ask to fill in the gaps of your strategy?

_____

Write out the details of your plan to ask him/her to join you in your journey:

When? _____

Where? _____

How? _____

Who meets the CLEAR requirements for a healthy and helpful relationship with you?

C - connect

L - learn

E - excited

A - authentic

R - reliable

_____

_____

4

HOW DOES GOD SEE YOU?

I know not everyone who reads this book believes there is a God.

Maybe you embrace the idea that there is a God or higher power, but the idea that God has any consideration for you at all seems like a far-off belief. No matter what you believe, keep reading. I am not going to spend my effort trying to convince you to believe any differently about God and His existence. However, I am going to push you beyond the sense of what you can simply see. I am going to provide you with ideas and principles which inherently reveal potential within yourself. You can sift through my beliefs, but don't sell yourself short on the truth of what works when discovering potential. Try tapping into your sense that there is something bigger going on in this world beyond what you and I can fully perceive.

If you could see it all right now in front of you, there would be no need for this book. For your efforts to find hidden potential you cannot yet see, it makes sense for you to tap into that which seems hidden beyond your own eyesight. If you do not believe in a God who holds the truth, then I am going

You were
so intricately
created that to
discover all that
is in you would
take a lifetime.

to ask you to at least consider the truths behind the principles I am about to explore. Put them to the test. See if they reveal something to you yet unseen. If you can begin to see the principles behind how God sees you, you can discover more hidden potential within yourself.

PRINCIPLE ONE:
There is always more undiscovered potential in you.

You are filled with more potential than you can comprehend. The hidden potential you have complements the being you are. It fits perfectly with your design. If God created you, then He knows you better than you know you. God sees you for who you are and who you are meant to be. He sees you more accurately than anyone. To God your potential is not incomprehensible or hidden; it is just yet to be discovered by you. You were so intricately created that to discover all that is in you, including your inherent potential, would take a lifetime.

I love the optimism in the poetry writings of the most successful and revered king of the ancient world, King David. He wrote of the knowledge of his Creator regarding the complex human design. Examine the positivity in this passage:

> *[A]You have searched me, Lord,*
> *and you know me.*
> *You know when I sit and when I rise;*
> *you perceive my thoughts from afar.*

[A] Psalm 139:1-3, 13-16

You discern my going out and my lying down;
  you are familiar with all my ways.
For you created my inmost being;
  you knit me together in my mother's womb.
I praise you because I am fearfully and wonderfully made;
  your works are wonderful,
  I know that full well.
My frame was not hidden from you
  when I was made in the secret place,
  when I was woven together in the depths of the earth.
Your eyes saw my unformed body;
  all the days ordained for me were written in your book
  before one of them came to be.

There is comfort and security in the idea that, if we cannot yet see something within ourselves, then someone who is close to us, whether a friend or higher power, is available to point out what we have yet to discover. The beauty behind the idea of God seeing you is that nothing remains hidden from His perspective of you. Your divine creator knows you in the most in-depth way. Getting to know God, then, provides access and insight into greater perspective and knowledge of oneself.

PRINCIPLE TWO:
There is more Godly potential inherent within you.

"You look just like your father." I have heard this statement for most of my life. Now my Dad is 6'4," almost completely bald and has a gray beard. I stand as tall as I can at 5'10," I keep the hair off my face and still on my head where it belongs. I know people do not think I look exactly like my father, but there are traits, facial features and mannerisms that are just like his. My sons are unique and yet much like their father. I have the one who leans towards leadership and organizes life into efficient systems, and one son who loves to crack jokes, have fun and get the party started. They both exhibit different parts of my personality and yet add all new features of their own. They are each unique, and yet both bear the image of their father.

Galileo once said the "Holy Ghost intended to teach us how to go to heaven, not how the heavens go." The calculations and detailed information regarding the universe and its creation is so immense that it is still beyond complete understanding. The first parts of the Bible reveal God created a world and a universe that is vast beyond human comprehension. It is something bigger than you and me. That being said, God gave you full commission to explore His creation. In the creation account, as written in the book of Genesis, the climax of the creation story is not when God created the heavens and earth, nor is it when God created the angels, nor is it when God created the vast beasts of the earth. The climax of the creation story occurs when God created you and me. You are the best part! A big reason you are the best part is because humans are the only beings created in the image of the Creator.

Just like my father, my sons and I share likenesses, there are traits of God within each human being. If you are created in the image of God, you share inherent traits of your Creator. Do you enjoy goodness, peace, beauty and color? It is because you are an image bearer of God. Do you like to take a holiday or a day off now and then? It is because you are an image bearer of God. Do you like to create, produce, organize, or manage? It is because you are an image bearer of God. Do you love, enjoy and care about that which you have produced? It is because you are an image bearer of God. The more you learn about God, the more you learn about yourself. One example of a trait you share with God at some level is creativity. When my children share that they are bored, I quickly remind them they are responsible for their own boredom. I further remind them they are created in the image of a creative God, ensuring they have some level of creativity inherent within them waiting to be released. The same is true for you. There are creativity, innovation and potential within you lying dormant, waiting to be unlocked and unleashed. This means your greatest idea has not yet been conceived. Your most creative invention, product or innovation is waiting for you to acknowledge its existence. There are worlds of creativity ready for your hands to design the intricacies within them. Unleashed creative potential feels wonderful when you build something new and meaningful with it. Creative potential was inherently placed within you, providing you with purpose and pleasure when you discover and use it for good.

There are creativity, innovation and potential within you lying dormant, waiting to be unlocked and unleashed. This means your greatest idea has not yet been conceived.

PRINCIPLE THREE:
There is more purposeful potential for you if you are truly ready for it.

While God knows all there is to know about you, it is not His goal to keep that information from you. He has great plans for you. God says in one of the more popular verses in the Bible, [B] *"For I know the plans I have for you," declares the Lord, "plans to prosper you and not to harm you, plans to give you hope and a future."* God created you with purpose and potential. He delights in revealing His purpose for your life along with the tools He placed within you to accomplish His purposes. God has more to show you, if you will let Him reveal it to you.

[C] King David had a sobering reality that God had more for him when instead David remained distracted in unworthy and eventually devastating pursuits. Because God had more to show David, he sent one of David's close friends, the prophet Nathan, to share God's truth with David. Nathan told David it was undeniable that God had blessed David with a crown to rule, defeated enemies, loyal subjects, a grand palace, a beautiful wife, and a growing kingdom. Then Nathan dropped a sledgehammer of truth upon David's life. He told David that God was even ready to give David more, but because David was lost in selfish, false and immoral pursuits, he would not be receiving further blessings. David would instead be enduring the consequences of his immoral, unethical and illegal actions.

This story has at some level haunted me and made me wonder if there was more God had ready to give me, but I have forfeited the blessing by my

[B] Jeremiah 29:11, [C] 2 Samuel 12

actions. Sometimes I will catch myself wondering why God has not revealed more to me or why He has not blessed me more. Perhaps the answer is that my mind and heart are not yet prepared to handle such a revelation or blessing. If God knows me, then He knows what I need and what I can handle. He knows when I am truly ready for Him to show me what I cannot yet see.

How about you? Are you ready to set aside distractions so God can show you the potential He has placed within you and the further blessings He has prepared for you to receive? If you are interested in seeing more of what God wants to show you, I encourage you to read a book I co-authored called *ReFocus: A Manageable Bible Reading Plan* available on Amazon. The book is a daily tool to help you focus or refocus on what God wants to show you. God has more for you if you are willing to see it.

PRINCIPLE FOUR:

There is more future potential ahead of you if you will move forward in faith to see it.

Stated another way, "God knows you, shows you, and grows you." Of course, if you let Him. While God has potential to reveal to us, He often includes a step for us to take in order to truly see it with our own eyes. The irony is that taking this step usually requires us to move forward without actually seeing first with our eyes.

Because of my macular dystrophy, I often have to step closer and closer towards an object in order for it to truly come into focus and understand what the object is. Before my eye condition, I could just squint and the object might come into focus without the requirement of drawing closer to it. Now, squinting does not work. It just makes things blurrier. I have to move forward in order to understand what is ahead of me. This is often scary, but it is required. This is the faith element. It is worth understanding that faith is not total blindness to the situation at hand. Faith means if my eyes cannot see, then what does my heart tell me? What does my head tell me? What does my gut tell me? The collective answers to those questions determines whether or not I am moving forward towards something I cannot yet see.

Your most creative invention, product or innovation is waiting for you to acknowledge its existence.

CHAPTER 4 SIMPLE STEPS:

1. Think about how much is unknown about the universe and how much is unknown about the micro universe. Think about the complexity of you. How much of you is still unknown to you? What amounts of powerful potential could possibly be tucked into your design? Write down your thoughts and feelings.

_____

_____

_____

_____

_____

2. List some common traits you see within every human being. What kind of potential does this create for you?

COMMON HUMAN TRAITS   POTENTIAL FOR ME

_____   _____

_____   _____

_____   _____

_____   _____

3. Write down attitudes or actions you are repetitively doing that could be hindering the revealing of potential in your life.

_____

_____

What could you do to diminish these behaviors and open yourself up to more positive possibilities?

_____

_____

4. Ask yourself, "What is the best next step for my future?" Now, contemplatively ask, "What does my heart tell me? What does my head tell me? What does my gut tell me?" Write down your answers.

HEART TELLS ME   HEAD TELLS ME   GUT TELLS ME

_____   _____   _____

_____   _____   _____

_____   _____   _____

_____   _____   _____

What common thread of ideas do you see?

_____

_____

If you want further clarity regarding your full and future potential, if you want to try moving forward with the idea that there is a God who knows you fully and is worth getting to know, then continue reading.

Sometimes the move forward is a single step. Sometimes it is a simple shift. Sometimes it is a leap. Seeing your undiscovered potential through God's eyes may be just one step away. Perhaps you sensed something greater is waiting for you. It is not actually that far ahead of you, but fear or circumstances have simply gotten in the way. Today is the perfect day for you to stretch your leg out and take a step. Maybe you do not know what that step looks like. That would be the first question to ask and resolve.

WHAT DOES IT LOOK LIKE TO TAKE A STEP FORWARD TO SEE WHAT GOD SEES?

Maybe it is talking to someone else who believes in God. Maybe it is reading or listening to something more about God. Maybe it is trying to talk directly to God by praying or writing down your thoughts. Maybe you know a better answer than what I am suggesting. What do your heart, head and gut say?

Maybe seeing your undiscovered potential through God's eyes is just a shift away. In other words, you are on the right path but you have just recently become sidetracked. You just need to set aside the distractions and get back in tune with God. You know what to do, because you have done it before; and the reality is you will probably have to do it again someday. The question is, "Will you make the adjustment now?" It is one thing to know you are off track and another to do nothing about it. Make the adjustment and see what potential is in store for you.

Maybe seeing your undiscovered potential through God's eyes feels like a leap away. It might mean walking through the door of a church building for the first time in a long time or opening a dusty Bible. It may start with wrestling with questions like, "Is God real? Does God really care about me? Does He have something better for me?" These are great questions to explore. I encourage you not to stop short of solid answers.

Whether it is a step, a shift or a leap taken, the adjustment will grow us. We will be farther ahead than when we started.

Another wonderful aspect King David realized about God is that when he would move forward in faith, God would go with him. In that same psalm quoted earlier David writes,

> D *Where can I go from your Spirit?*
> *Where can I flee from your presence?*
> *If I go up to the heavens, you are there;*
> *if I make my bed in the depths, you are there.*
> *If I rise on the wings of the dawn,*
> *if I settle on the far side of the sea,*
> *even there your hand will guide me,*
> *your right hand will hold me fast.*

D Psalm 139:7-10 - ESV

God will grow us by challenging us to move forward in faith, and He will go with us, guiding us as we eventually meet the challenge. Before long, His purposes and your potential become visible. The truth of who you are and who you are meant to be becomes undeniable. Then you can give credit to God like so many others before you saying, "I once was blind, but now I see."

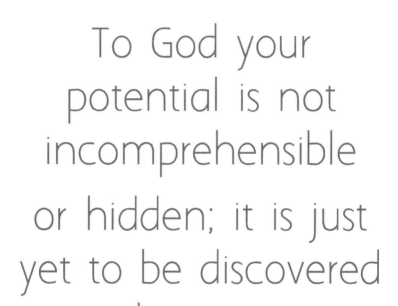

To God your potential is not incomprehensible or hidden; it is just yet to be discovered by you.

HOW TO KEEP YOUR EYES WIDE OPEN

Hopefully, you attempted to investigate how you see you, how others see you and how God sees you.

Uncovering your hidden potential is a process. While some realizations will come suddenly, most of the potential you will want to pursue will reveal itself over time. The digging, discovering and discerning your next best move will take a while if done well. It will feel more like a journey than an instant teleportation to success and a better version of yourself. So, here are some important tips and guidelines along the way.

ONE: DON'T STOP DREAMING

"Your child easily becomes lost and distracted during class lessons and discussions."

"Your child needs to develop better listening skills in class as he sometimes drifts away from us."

"Your child tends to daydream."

I was looking back at my elementary school report cards, and I found a running theme. And those quotes were just from second grade. My teacher, Miss Gagliardo, was quite concerned how I would turn out. It's all good Miss G., because dreaming is good. It is a necessary skill in success and in leadership and discovering your potential. With dreams, comes vision. With vision, comes change. With change, comes progress.

Dreaming opens our eyes wide to see what could be. Sometimes the dreams are about adding, and sometimes they are about subtracting. What I mean is, sometimes you dream about what your world would look like if you had a certain possession, resource, relationship, skill, or ability. Other times you dream about what your world would look like if you could just rid it of a dilemma, a particular type of person or behavior, a weakness or temptation, a crime, or evil. Both types of dreams, whether based on desire or discontent, can lead to new vision, new purpose and new potential.

> Dreaming opens our eyes wide to see what could be.

There was a leadership void in one of our growing ministries at my church that happened to fall under my supervision. There were other potential leaders, but they needed more time to develop. So, I offered to fill the leadership gap for nine months with two potential leaders by my side ready to learn and eventually succeed me as leader of this ministry. Because I had recently inherited this particular ministry under my oversight and was unfamiliar with its procedures, this would be a crash course for me when it came to the details and workings of this ministry. However, I knew there were smarter people than I already involved who had a strong passion for this ministry program I was "not leading." I quickly involved those smarter people. Now that I had smarter people involved, I needed to find a smart vision in order to move this ministry forward to the next level of its growth. In one of the first meetings I led, I asked the smart, connected people in the room, "What needs to be better within this ministry?" It was as if they were standing ready with built up frustrations that could not wait any longer to be revealed and released. I filled an entire, big white board with their answers to the question. After about twenty minutes of listening and writing down everything that was wrong with the inner workings of this ministry, I took a red dry-erase marker and wrote the words, "Praise God!" over the already written answers. This was an opportunity to explain that we now had vision. We could see plenty of areas to work on that would improve the ministry. We knew what the ministry needed to look like if it were going to grow to the next level. It needed to look better. And we knew and identified what was keeping it from currently looking great. Praise God! We had vision and ideas. I also explained to a somewhat perplexed room that, since we could now see it, we were going to be the ones to help bring about the needed adjustments. Someone shared with me long ago that if God gives you the vision, then it is your mission to bring it to fruition. It was also worth noting that we had a lot of new vision on that white board. We would need to turn problems into a plan with prioritized steps. We could also rest assured that because of the number of needed improvements, our leadership responsibilities would

Vision is always around the corner.

You just need to know how to look for it.

not be running dry anytime soon. The next part of our meeting was strategy based, as we identified which part of the vision to implement first.

Vision is always around the corner. You just need to know how to look for it. Letting our minds drift off into dreams only opens our brain's receptors to see more of what could be or what could be improved. So, don't stop dreaming.

TWO: STAY THE STUDENT

One of my staff once asked me a great question. She said, "What happens when I run out of great ideas." She had only been on the job for a few months. She was innovative and bringing new insight to the table. She was also smart enough to know this will not always be the case. At some point, her opinions and previous experience will not seem fresh and amazing. Then what? What if she cannot live up to the current hype? I assured her I did not hire her because of her great ideas and perspectives. That was just a bonus. I hired her because of the potential I saw in her and her quick ability to learn. I told her, "This is why we spend so much time learning leadership skills now, because you will need them in the future." Good leaders know that sometimes the vision and the ideas run out. Good leadership skills include the ability to learn, because great leaders are learners.

Something I am continually learning is that it is always smart to play the student. Have you ever gone to a seminar, conference, workshop or retreat

Playing the role of the student means shelving your accomplishments to focus on acquiring new information.

for the purpose of learning something new; and you spent most of your brain energy trying to convince yourself and others that you already know a lot? The temptation when faced with a learning opportunity can be to dismiss its need before you ever consider the ideas available. Sometimes, it is easier to share a bunch of statements about why you or your organization is on the ball, rather than opening up to the opportunity for improvement. The desire is to be known as the expert in your field rather than the student who has yet to arrive. The irony is, experts are often intentionally playing the role of a student in order to see new possibilities and potential in their fields.

Playing the role of the student means asking lots of questions without showing off too many answers. It means spending your time learning rather than bragging. It requires more listening and note taking than talking. Playing the role of the student means shelving your accomplishments to focus on acquiring new information. If you slip into bragging rights, then learning becomes limited. Good information gets dismissed because you found a way to label the other person's perspective as inconsequential.

There is another side to the achievement or bragging coin. Because you may not feel you have accomplished anything note-worthy to date, you may deem yourself unworthy to even enter into a learning conversation. Still the best role to take in these situations is the role of the student. Then you avoid being a jerk, or a critic, or a scaredy cat. When you play the role of the student, you can ask all the questions you want while learning a ton in the moment, without having to filter anything out upfront. You make the other person who is sharing feel good, and in turn he/she will also think well of you. You can always learn something from someone. However, sometimes it takes a little more digging. So, as a student of learning, bring on the questions and gain new wisdom, insight and perspective.

THREE: COUNT ON CURVEBALLS

Several years ago, there was a movie starring Clint Eastwood and Amy Adams called Trouble with the Curve. It was about a baseball recruiter and his relationship with his daughter. During the movie, the father-daughter duo examines a minor league slugger over whom all the other recruiters are drooling. (Spoiler Alert) In the end, Amy Adams and Clint decide not to offer him a major-league contract because they observe what no other recruiters have noticed. He cannot hit a curve ball. It throws him into confusion, and he is not able to compensate to connect his bat with the ball. As great a hitter as this player is, an opposing pitcher will easily be able to shut him down once he discovers this slugger's Kryptonite, the curve ball.

Curve balls are a part of life and a part of the journey of unlocking new potential. You don't expect them; that is why they are curve balls. I observed that the most consistently successful individuals reserve time and leave emotional capital to deal with problems and dilemmas. They expect the unexpected. Wise people know they cannot predict everything that will come their way; so, they leave room for adjustments.

While curve balls will be thrown, it takes a major-league player to hit one. You can tell a major-league hitter from a player consistently stuck in the minor leagues of life. The minor leaguers are upset there is such a thing as a curve ball and that it is allowed to exist. They claim it is not fair. They find themselves upset a curve ball was thrown at them in the first place. And as a result, they consistently strike out. They may slam their bat on the ground or yell at the pitcher or umpire, but they are still out. They waste their time complaining and trying to defer blame. As a result, they accomplish nothing. It's like falling into a ditch. You can work your way out of the ditch; or you can just be angry that a ditch exists, and you fell into it. Some individuals attempt to analyze why they ended up in the ditch in the first place. That is a great exercise, but only to do after you are out of the ditch. If you are still in a ditch, all your current efforts and energy should be spent trying to get out. Then you can analyze all you want, and maybe even pout or be angry. I recommend you practice ditch dodging.

> Never
> solve
> a problem
> alone

In your search for potential, expect the unexpected. Expect problems and be ready to deal with them. Don't get angry or analytical. Deal with the problem and move forward. Here is a secret to becoming a great problem solver. Never solve a problem alone. Use the power, synergy, brilliance and wisdom that comes from a team of people around you, who care about you and enjoy solving problems together. The more minds at work on a problem, the increased probability of landing on a great solution.

When you can identify problems to solve—making sure they are problems that can be solved—then several brains working on a solution have a great chance at success. When more than one person owns the solution, it brings about teamwork when implementing the solution. Overall, it is better to identify problems to solve together.

Here is another truth about problems and curve balls. When you deal with them, they can make you sharper and stronger. If the journey were not tough, it would not be transforming. The hard obstacles in life, once tackled and removed, leave the greatest paths open.

Have you ever hated and loved the same thing at one time? It was a few years back that I decided I would run my first 5K race. It would be, like many Americans, running the epic Turkey Trot. For the couple of years prior, I watched and cheered my father as he ran the race and crossed the finish line. The thought occurred to me that if my father in his early 50s could run the race, I in my early 30s at the time could do it as well. So, I did. I started running. I never liked running. In fact, I hated it. And I still hate it. I remember the first time I tried to run around my block. I barely survived. It was embarrassing. My body had no idea what I was trying to do because I had never done it before. Over time my body could run one mile without stopping, then two miles and then eventually the 3.1 miles required for a 5K race. I hated running every day for the two months prior to the Turkey Trot, but I loved the feeling when I was done. And I loved the feeling of crossing that finish line on Thanksgiving Day that year, so much so that I continued to run. I ended up signing up for another 5K in December and then another one in January. I ran several 5K races that year. I built up my running tolerance to more than 6 miles without stopping. I was in some of the best shape of my life that year. And I ran the next year's Turkey Trot beating my time from the previous year. I hated running, and I still do. In fact, I still run now and then, but never like I did that year. The hate overpowered a bit of the love enough that I no longer run every day. But no worries, I found another hate and love activity in my life.

I now hate getting up while it is still dark, because I am by no means a morning person. I hate opening my garage to the cold morning air and letting in my workout partner, Raul, better known as Dr. Serrano. When a health doctor said he needed a workout buddy in the morning and wanted to know if I was interested, I hated to love to say yes. I hate when we begin the intense workout. I hate when it is almost over, but it is not yet over; and Raul pushes me to push myself to my limits. No joke, I almost passed out the first time we did this routine. I had to lie on the pavement outside my garage and pray for the world to stop spinning while Raul did the other half of the routine by himself. I hated it. But I love it when it is over. I love how the rest of my day goes. I love the results I see and feel physically and the friendship it is building relationally. When my alarm goes off in the dark morning, I hate and love to work out.

That is how it often feels when really digging in to discover your potential. Hard truths about yourself and others rise to the surface, and they are tough to handle. Tough times provide opportunities for you to learn the most and grow your strongest. If tough times grow you stronger, then trying to avoid tough times can actually make you weaker.

> Tough times provide opportunities for you to learn the most and grow your strongest.

I was invited on a mission trip to India. I was there to teach Indian pastors and be one of the key speakers for a Christian rally the Indian churches in the area put on over several nights. One of my favorite memories of that trip was the night I was speaking, and the power went out, and then moments later came back on. My interpreter started coughing uncontrollably. He tried to regain his composure but struggled as if something was stuck in his throat. Eventually he got back in the swing of things. I made some light-hearted comments which he then translated to the audience. They erupted in laughter. I thought to myself I'm killing it. I am hilarious in India. I found out later that the reason they were laughing was because the interpreter explained to them that when the lights went out he accidentally swallowed a fly. He was actually killing it in India.

While on the trip my companions and I were treated to a ride on an elephant. It was awesome. We later found out this was rare since the elephant we rode on was a temple elephant. This meant he was rarely ridden and often shown off at Hindu parades. I later learned that elephant riding was a somewhat sore subject among the Indian people. The activity used to be more common and accepted in India. What changed was animal rights groups from the Western hemisphere getting involved in Indian politics to try to ban elephant riding. The Indian people I interacted with were very open about their feelings toward western animal rights groups. Of all the awful ideas and unhelpful contributions from America, this seemed to offend them the worst. This was the reasoning communicated to me by the Indian people. "The animal rights groups are killing our elephants!" they claimed. Not on purpose, of course. The irony is these groups have fought for so many rules in the name of protecting the elephants from any type of labor that the elephants are no longer getting enough exercise. The Indian elephants are now getting sick more easily and dying at earlier ages. They are protected from tough situations where their bodies can build up strength and immunities. Protecting the elephants is actually killing them. I could not believe it. But it made sense. And I can see the parallels. Tough situations are meant to make you grow stronger. Avoiding or protecting yourself from work, pain, toil or trials only makes you weaker. You and I need the curve balls; they teach us and toughen us up. They make us sharper, stronger and better able to see and achieve our potential.

FOUR: LIVE OUT LOUD

When you were a kid, did you wonder with anticipation what you were going to get for Christmas? Maybe you still do, like I do. Did you wonder, "Will I get that for which I have been asking?" Have you ever discovered your gifts before Christmas? I know some people who try to find their gifts early. Have you accidentally found your presents? I remember a time playing hide and seek while growing up. I hid in my mother's closet. I discovered a Louisville Slugger baseball bat somewhat hidden in the closet. My first thought was, "I did not know that Mom plays baseball." A few weeks later I unwrapped that same baseball bat on Christmas morning. It was not until then that it all clicked in my head. For some reason, I found it more believable that Mom led a secret life where she would sneak out of the house and play semi-professional baseball and be back in time for dinner or breakfast.

I still get excited about Christmas. There is an energy in the air as the holiday grows closer. I still wonder what new gifts I will discover. Life is full of hope for the future. It is okay to get excited with anticipation. What new goals will be achieved? What kind of expansion will happen? What new gifts will you discover? What positive life change will take place? What greatness does the future hold? What new potential will I see? The journey to your potential is exciting. So, get excited about it.

I was sitting by a pond one day watching as what appeared to be a single fish leaping over and over out of water. I thought to myself, "Why does the fish keep leaping out of his protected environment?" And then I came up with my own answer. All the fish knows is the pond, but there is an excitement in experiencing a world beyond the borders of the pond. I bet he loves experiencing this world so much, even if for only a brief moment. I bet he can't get enough of it. I bet he is addicted to trying to experience another world even if for only a few seconds.

I get it. There have been those brief moments in my life, and I'm sure still are, when I feel I am experiencing something beyond this world. I sense something bigger than what my eyes can see in front of me, and it radiates down to my soul. I get it. I can't get enough, so I pursue those experiences even if they are only brief and rare. I long for the day when I am not bound by the borders of this life's pond. In the meantime, I cannot help excitedly pursuing something greater than myself. In this pursuit, I also find I cannot keep it to myself. It is okay, and even encouraged, for you to let the world around you know when you are experiencing something profound in your journey. It is expected of you, because you were created to share such excitements.

SHARING A STORY

It was less than twenty-four hours after our daughter, Avri, was born. We were in the hospital room—just my wife, Avri and I. Erica and I were admiring our daughter and all the funny faces and noises she was making. Then it happened. All of a sudden Avri stopped breathing. To this day I do not know what caused this occurrence. She took a breath in, but then she stopped. We waited for a scream. We waited for a sound. We waited for anything to happen. But nothing was happening. Her lips started to turn blue. Her skin became pale. My soul cried out to God begging Him to make her breathe, to exhale, to cry, to do something. But nothing was happening.

Each moment that passed seemed like an eternity, until it finally happened. She screamed out. Her lips grew red, and her complexion restored. She cried out, and it was the most beautiful sound to my ears. The scare was over. She started breathing again. My heart rejoiced because her life, and your life, and everyone's life is meant to make a noise. That is the purpose. We were created to live in such a way that our lives scream out an acknowledgment of the power of life itself.

Let your life scream out passion. It is difficult to be quiet when you are passionate about something. So, live out loud so the world can hear your passion. Let those around you know when you have discovered new potential for your life and how you live it. Get passionate. Get loud. Let the world know what and/or whom you love and care about. Your life was meant to make a noise.

Live out loud so the world can hear your passion.

Your life was always meant to make a noise.

CHAPTER 5 SIMPLE STEPS:

1. Out of the four guidelines, circle the one that feels easiest to implement.
   - Don't Stop Dreaming
   - Stay the Student
   - Count on Curveballs
   - Live Out Loud

Why do you think this one will be the easiest?

_____

_____

_____

_____

Which one feels like the most difficult to implement? Why?

_____

_____

_____

_____

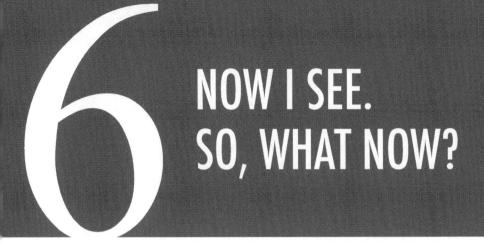

NOW I SEE.
SO, WHAT NOW?

Once you start seeing your potential,
it is time to begin developing a plan to achieve it.

While this is an ongoing process which reveals more and more as you journey ahead, perhaps there are already results from your efforts. Perhaps you can hear rumblings of a dragon awakening. If you are discovering new ideas, new dreams, new possible ventures, new skills to be developed, and new potential, then the next step is to begin achieving that potential. As with any journey, it will be difficult to try to do it by yourself. Consider gaining some assistance along the way. Maybe you already have a great mentor, coach or strong circle of friends who can cheer you on and are willing to dissect your problems and opportunities along the way. If this is not the case for you, then consider using some of our tools and services.

As an ordained and experienced pastor in a growing church, I help people who feel lost or stuck in life. I am also a certified and skilled life and leadership coach. I have authored several books and materials to guide people forward with ease into a successful and hopeful future. I see myself as a "potentialist." My life's work is dedicated to helping people see and achieve their potential through simple steps. It would be my pleasure to continue the journey with you as you pursue your potential.

Whichever path you choose to see and achieve your potential, I wish for you the best, for you to be blessed and for you to enjoy your success.

Connect with me at TomGoodlet.com where you'll find additional resources, workshops and one-on-one mentoring.

CHAPTER 6 SIMPLE STEPS:

1. Decide which of these three perspectives will be the first you want to develop further:
    - How you see yourself
    - How others see you
    - How God sees you

What steps will you take in the next three days to move forward?

_____

_____

2. Write down any stirring dragons you sense within. What potential have you spotted so far? What do the powerful possibilities look like for your life?

_____

_____

3. Enlist extra help along the way. Make sure you have a mentor or coach in your corner to cheer you on and guide you when you feel stuck.

My mentor or coach will be ... _____

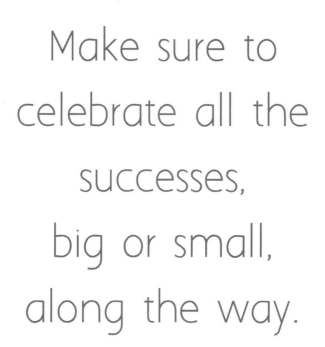

Make sure to
celebrate all the
successes,
big or small,
along the way.

CELEBRATE SUCCESS

Make sure to celebrate all the successes, big or small, along the way. Celebration takes time. It is often hard to slow down. There is something I have noticed about school buses. School buses force us to stop, to wait for kids, to slow down. We all do it because the cost of not stopping for kids getting on or off a bus is too great. We need more 'school bus' perspective in our lives. We need to slow down and celebrate. It is easy to get lost in trying to improve—always looking at and discussing what needs improvement, but successful individuals make sure to stop and take moments to celebrate success. The truth is there will always be ways to improve but there will not always be time to acknowledge and celebrate the wins. If we don't schedule or carve out time to celebrate, then it will never happen. Celebration can lead to inspiration and motivation. Lack of celebration leads to burn out. Take the time to reward your growth.

When one person sees a potential success or reveals a win, it inspires others to join the celebration. One of my favorite cities to visit is Greenville, South Carolina. In the heart of downtown Greenville there is an eye-catching bridge that overlooks the Reedy River Falls. The history of the bridge is almost as fascinating as the bridge itself.

Because of an economic boom within the city in 1960, a four-lane bridge, the Camperdown Bridge, was constructed. This new structure would allow workers to more easily commute to the city. The problem was this bridge now blocked the Reedy River Falls from view. Soon after the construction of this bridge, property values went down and the crime rate went up. It was in 1967 that a women's gardening club began sprucing up acreage around the falls. The women pulled weeds and planted flowers. They even raised funds for future beautification of the acres surrounding the falls. Over the following decades more and more landscaping took place until 1990 when an architect proposed making the beautiful park and public gardens around the falls a centerpiece for downtown. The problem of the Camperdown Bridge blocking the falls from view remained. In 2001, despite the charge from critics that removing the bridge would cause extra traffic jams in the city, the City Council voted to spend $1 million to tear down the four-lane bridge. From there the city spent $4.5 million and 14 months to build a pedestrian bridge that would frame and accentuate the falls and their beauty. This newly-named Liberty Bridge was an innovation of architecture that would later earn awards and prestige. Overall, the project cost $13 million dollars. Within two years of its completion it brought around $100 million in private investments around its location. Housing prices went up and crime went down. The City of Greenville had financial stability and growth that helped propel them forward even through the financial crisis of 2008.

It is amazing what a bit of beauty revealed can do. It was the collective vision of a few women who saw the beauty and potential in something enough to slowly and consistently reveal it for what it could be. And it blessed an entire city.

When you see a success in progress, celebrate it, even if it is still a success in the making. Then everyone wins, because potential inspires not just you, but also those around you. Celebrate your potential and watch your world change for the better.

Potential is around and within you. You just need to clearly see it. Recognizing it starts you on the journey to achieve it. Achieving your potential inspires others to achieve theirs. A life of lived-out potential is a purpose-filled life that brings out the best in you and others.

A life of lived-out potential is a purpose-filled life that brings out the best in you and others.

A LITTLE BIT MORE ABOUT
THE AUTHOR

Tom Goodlet is a husband, a father and a forever student of Jesus Christ.

He is married to his beautiful wife Erica and has two boys, Parker and Mason, and a little girl, Avri. He is currently the Associate Minister at Harborside Christian Church in Safety Harbor, FL. Prior to his tenure at Harboside he was in full time youth ministry for 11 years. Tom has a Bachelors of Science in Communications from Milligan College in East Tennessee and a Masters of Arts in Theological Studies from Liberty University. Tom grew up just outside of NYC in Hicksville (nothing hick about it), Long Island. Tom loves humor, adventure and Jesus.

Over the past few years Tom became a best-selling author of multiple books and earned his Life Coach certification. He became certified as a Leader Effectiveness Training instructor through Gordon Training International, where he equips organizations to build a positive work culture with increased productivity and profitability. He has decades of experience as a motivational speaker, teacher and professional mentor. Tom is also the Co-Host of the Potentialist Podcast. Along with the help of Co-Host Dr. Raul Serrano, this podcast helps listeners understand there is still more in you, more for you and more to be done through you. This podcast is available on iTunes, SoundCloud, TuneIn and other popular podcast websites and applications.

For more access to Tom Goodlet's books, workshops and one-on-one mentoring, or to book Tom for your organization's next engagement please visit www.TomGoodlet.com.

51535058R10063

Made in the USA
Columbia, SC
23 February 2019